What people are saying about..

Alone But Not Lonely

"Donna Schaper's concise Scriptural meditations offer both comfort and challenge to women of prayer and practical action. In every season, her reflections are helpful in their honesty about us and our limits and in their down-to-earth wisdom."

Pamela Smith, SS.C.M.
Author, *Days of Dust and Ashes*

"When Donna Schaper tells a story, there is always more than meets the eye. Start out in her vegetable garden, or a crowded airport, or at a kitchen table, and end up in the presence of God. But never a predictable God."

Patrick Marrin
Editor, *Celebration*

"These reflections convey the vulnerability, the limits and the infinite depths of the human spirit. With gentle strength they present a message sought by many today: How to move from a deep fear of loneliness by connecting with God, community, and self to the solitude in which we encounter our true strength."

Dr. Audrey Doetzel, NDS
Director, Relation and Encounter

"This book not only describes solitude; it enables us to experience it through the author's insights into Scripture, her personal joys and struggles, and her skillful quotation of wise spiritual teachers."

Evan Drake Howard
Author, *Suffering Loss, Seeking Healing*

"These meditations deal straightforwardly and honestly with both solitude and loneliness, linking the daily experiences of wife, mother, and minister to Scripture and prayer. I found this an affirming and nurturing companion for my own daily prayer."

Margot Hover, D.Min.
Author, *Caring for Yourself While Caring for Others*

"This is a woman who knows her inner self. In her solitude, Donna Schaper has reflected on many common themes. On the dilemma of parenting, she writes poignantly, 'We should not let them go. We must let them go. They need to have their own adventures so they can get to their own solitude.' This is a beautifully written book to take into your own solitude."

Judy Esway
Author, *Real Life, Real Spirituality*

"I commend this book for those who are grieving or lonely for any reason, as a daily companion and a wise friend."

Celia Allison Hahn
Director, Churches Nourishing a Spirituality for the World

"The 'everydayness' of Donna's work is what makes it so appealing. The pains and joys, the defeats and triumphs that she relates—and helps us learn from—are the pieces of daily life that ordinary people experience. That she is able to do this with both wisdom and humor makes this book a special gift."

Nancy D. Richardson
Harvard University Divinity School

"This tender book—which combines Scripture, story, and prayer—reminds us of the important distinction between loneliness and solitude and brings God's love and grace into the center of our daily lives."

The Rev. Dr. Andrea Ayvazian
Mount Holyoke College

Alone but *not* Lonely

A Spirituality of Solitude

DONNA E. SCHAPER

TWENTY-THIRD PUBLICATIONS
Mystic, CT 06355

Twenty-Third Publications
185 Willow Street
P.O. Box 180
Mystic, CT 06355
(860) 536-2611
(800) 321-0411

ISBN: 0-89622-956-4
Library of Congress Catalog Card Number: 98-75051
Printed in the U.S.A.

Dedication

**To Carrie Tidlund,
who lived alone but not lonely**

Contents

Introduction..1

1. The Temptation..4

2. Removing the Clutter..................................6

3. The Capacity to Mourn...............................8

4. The Enemy Is "Control"............................11

5. Feeling All Alone.......................................13

6. The Weight of Things 15

7. Spiritual Rock Gardens.............................18

8. Needing Friends 20

9. Nothing Is Perfect....................................22

10. From the Inside Out................................24

11. The Heavy Becomes Light.......................26

12. Time for God..29

13. The Place of Prayer 31

14. We Need Time Alone 33

15. Time Together 36

16. Feeling Powerless 38

17. We Are Not God.......................................40

18. Hungry People...42

19. Far Away from Home 44

20. Dealing with Our Fears..............................47

21. Fixing Broken Glass 49

22. Focusing on God 51

23. Remembering Saves Us..............................53

24. We Are All "Different" 55

25. Trust Can Open Doors 57

26. Take Nothing for the Journey 59

27. Sharing Holy Food 61

28. A Salute to Stillness...............................63

29. Living Our Own Lives 65

30. Friends with Jesus 68

31. God's Beautiful Sculpture........................70

32. Believing in Angels 73

33. Jesus was Fully Present........................75

34. The Paradox of Faith 77

35. Believing in Miracles.............................79

Alone But Not Lonely

Introduction

*W*hat is the difference between solitude and loneliness? One we choose; the other we are chosen by. Many of us ache for the pleasures of solitude: we need to "get away," be "by ourselves," think our own thoughts and dream our own dreams. I confess to sometimes walking in the mall as though I'm shopping. I'm not. I'm remembering what I forgot. I am enjoying solitude. No one has my phone number in the mall.

Loneliness comes to me as often as solitude. I speak, but even my intimates don't hear what I say. I look around but don't see the wonder of what is there. Things look gray. The next day, under the same weather conditions, they might look beautiful again. Loneliness is when we get trapped deep inside and can't get out. Loneliness happens to everyone.

It is good for us to explore both solitude and loneliness. Both offer solace. Both. Each is part of the other. Think of Mary who came to the garden alone (Jn 20:15–18). First, she is deeply lonely. The whole world is lonely that early Easter morning. Then Jesus speaks to her, and her loneliness turns to solitude. An encounter with Jesus lets Mary be by herself in a different way. It also opens her to companionship in a different way. Solitude brings us back to people and to God!

I love the song "I Come to the Garden Alone." It expresses a certain solace in being alone. It describes and makes us feel the sorrow and the joy that Mary felt. And we feel it right along with her. We feel her hope, too. Though Jesus left her bereft on Good Friday, he has returned on Easter Sunday. Through an experience of communion with Jesus in solitude, hope can be restored and renewed.

Those of us who glimpse the power of the resurrection know what is going on in the garden. We are risking our hope intentionally—on a kind of cross. We are risking it so that we may have it. The theologian Chris Smith says this is the path of Jesus: "The resurrected one went to the cross on Good Friday," meaning that it was Jesus' own decision that made the resurrection possible.

We have to risk as Jesus did if our own hope is to endure. We have to give ourselves time for solitude and we have to allow ourselves to be alone. The reflections in this book are about risking hope through the solace of both solitude and loneliness. They are meant for you if you are looking to renew your relationship with Jesus. They are meant for you if you feel helpless in the face of all the suffering and evil in our world. They are meant to convince you that you are not alone and yet you must sometimes stand on your own. Understanding this paradox is the difference between loneliness and solitude.

The specific intention of these reflections is to empower you to pray for the gift of hope for yourself first of all.

Often we pray only for others and neglect our own needs, weaknesses, and capacities. In giving service to others, we can become very lonely. In caring for ourselves and others, we can find solitude.

The image of Mary in the garden alone is a very positive one for us in precisely these terms. She is praying for the return of her savior and she is praying for herself. The reflections in this book are meant to encourage you to pray too, and to find the time to be alone in the garden where you can wait, listen to, and respond to your savior.

CHAPTER ONE

The Temptation

Moses sent them to spy on the land of Canaan…and they cut down from there a single branch of grapes and they carried it on a pole between them… They also brought some pomegranates and figs… (Numbers 13:17, 23).

*B*ecause of the enormous effect that advertising has on us, consciously or unconsciously, we are prone to enjoying our estrangement from God more than we should. We enjoy the "wild grapes" of our Exodus. We become strangers to ourselves because we imagine that we should be different or better than we are. Canaan's grapes are so large: ours are so small.

We need to learn how to look beyond the advertised messages that tempt us to be other than we are. Be beautiful, they tell us—as though we are not fine in the eyes of God. Be thin, they command—as though only thin people can experience love and joy. Reward yourself, they advise—as though more and more possessions will make us happy. Scripture assures us that we are not the first to desire the "grapes" of Canaan, not the first to be estranged from our best selves or the love of God. The people of Israel looked longingly to the grapes and pomegranates—and sometimes to the gods—just over the border, and they assumed that the ones over there were better and more pleasing.

But isn't it true that even when we yield to the temptation to want more or be more, we still feel very lonely? We stand in front of a mirror and don't like the one we see. We are tempted to search for more and better ways to be someone we are not, to be anyone but the one we are, anyone but the person so lovingly created by God. We have to remember that God puts grapes on our side of the border, too.

When we learn to love ourselves as we are, solitude at the mirror is a wonderful experience. We understand that we are what we are. We are God's. We may still be tempted to want a better, improved version of ourselves, but we can turn that temptation into a friend, a goal, a hope—rather than a condemnation. We can refuse the temptation to judge ourselves against false images. With the grace of God we can accept who we are and see great beauty there.

My Prayer...

Help me, Creator God, to resist the temptation to be what I am not. Let me be me—as you have created me. Help me to enjoy the "grapes" in my own yard, knowing that they are very good indeed. Amen.

CHAPTER TWO

Removing the Clutter

I planted, Apollos watered, but God gave the growth. So neither the one who plants nor the one who waters is anything, but only God who gives the growth (I Corinthians 3: 6,7).

Sometimes spiritual solitude feels like the dog days of summer. We're too weary, too spent to do what needs to be done. In late summer, when the asters are standing on the toes of the daisies, and the grapes have twisted on to the bittersweet vine, we have no ambition to sort them out again. Early in the season we are energetic and enthusiastic; of course the impatiens will not be invaded by the spearmint! We assume that we will keep ahead of the weeds, but we never quite do.

In the spiritual life, we begin our journey toward clarity and growth many times, much as we begin again in the fall to clear the garden of summer clutter. We renew our hope that we can grow spiritually and achieve the kind of solitude that will energize us. We start out with zest, fasting, praying, and doing good works. But then we stall. We may even have forgotten that it is God who gives the growth. We may have forgotten to rely on God, and our goal may no longer be clear.

E.L. Doctorow has said that writing a novel is like driving a car at night. "You can see only as far as your headlights but you can also make the whole trip that way." Often we want an imperial clarity—we want to see the whole picture. But this is impossible. Clarity for the day, not the season, should be our goal. We grow little by little, day by day, in God's own time.

It's true, of course, that we will sometimes falter. The weeds sometimes outpace the flowers in our spiritual gardens. But this can be good. We sometimes have to abandon our large goals and consider smaller ones instead. We have to plant less and rely more on God for our growth.

Instead of absolute clarity, we sometimes have to settle for "haze." We can learn to love it. Haze has its own benefits. It keeps us clear about our incompleteness and our need for God.

My Prayer...

Creator God, who makes everything grow, help me to grow one step at a time, no more, no less. Give me the courage to plant and to water, but then to wait for you to give the growth. Amen.

CHAPTER THREE

The Capacity to Mourn

"The hour is now coming, indeed it has come, when you will be scattered, and you will leave me alone. Yet I am not alone because the Father is with me…" (John 16:32,33).

*W*e can be alone but not alone at the same time. We can be all by ourselves and God can still be with us. Solitude differs from loneliness. We are accompanied by God in the first and forget God's presence in the second. Mourners know the difference. The beloved is gone but God is near.

Jesus knew about the presence of God. He predicts that his hour will come, but that God, the one he calls Father, will be with him in his suffering.

We can suffer alone in fear. Or we can suffer in solitude, believing that God is with us. The great essayist Montaigne once wrote: "deprive death of its strangeness....let us frequent it; let us get used to it." The same can be said for solitude.

Two of my childhood friends died early, one in a

snowbank at eighteen on the New York State Thruway, the other after catching my pitches in a softball game. She had an aneurysm in her brain. It took her away, and she never came back. We were both thirteen. I missed both these friends in a kind of adolescent grief that bore loneliness deep inside me. Only later, as someone who deals often with grief, have I learned that we can grow in the midst of grieving. I am able to testify to others and accompany them. I know that the loneliness of grief is not permanent. I know a bit of what Jesus knew: that when our hour comes to suffer, the Spirit of God also comes along.

Many people live lonely lives because they don't know how to befriend their suffering. They don't see the Spirit in the suffering. They shut down in loneliness. Solitude will only come when they say yes to the suffering, and let go of how things "should" have been.

Life itself teaches us that we will not only experience the death and loss of those we love; we ourselves will also die. The truth about the Spirit's presence in suffering applies to our own deaths too.

Sherwin Nuland in his book *How We Die* urges us to cross the finish line with great zest. He appreciates the fact that many of us simply die from old age. We become "worn and torn"; we have been programmed to cave in. "The very old do not succumb to disease; they implode their way into eternity."

Thomas Jefferson thought the same, "There is a ripeness of time for death…when it is reasonable we should drop off, and make room for another growth. When we have lived our generation out, we should not wish to encroach on another." Old people often say, "I'm ready to die." They mean that they have robbed death of its strangeness. They are comfortable with solitude. They have learned about the presence of the Spirit.

The sweet peas in my garden are teaching me the meaning of this and how suffering plays a part in our growth. For years I have planted sweet peas and they have not come up. They sprout two little leaves and then they stop growing. Something underneath is wrong, down deep in the soil.

But this year, I have planted sweet peas again. I also loaded the soil with enough manure to fertilize five gardens. I am learning that growth requires hard work and some suffering, and a great deal of patience. I am willing to wait for my flowers in solitude.

All of us will know frustration, or failure, or even great grief in our lifetimes. But when we know we're not alone, we'll get through it.

My Prayer...

Let me not be afraid to mourn, O God. Let me not be a stranger either to death or to hope, and let me always count on your companionship on both sides of the finish line. If you can't turn my grief to joy, then at least turn my loneliness to solitude. Amen.

CHAPTER FOUR

The Enemy Is "Control"

"See here! For three years I have come looking for fruit on this fig tree, and still I find none. Cut it down! Why should it be wasting this soil?" The gardener replied, "Sir, let it alone for one more year, until I dig around it and put manure on it. If it bears fruit next year, well and good; but if not, you can cut it down" (Luke 13: 7–9).

Gardens and the grief of loneliness have the same enemy: control. We can only do so much, then we have to step back and trust. We quickly learn this when we love others (and when we tend gardens). With love, as with crops, control is the thing we have to fear most. We can manure our gardens completely, but we can't extract guarantees of produce from the soil. Figs do not grow on our command.

Neither can we command ourselves not to feel loneliness. We can't get rid of it the way we might rid our kitchens of dirt. Loneliness may linger even after all our best efforts to get rid of it. But if we go after our loneliness with a lighter touch, we may find solitude and even

11

clarity. We don't control these things. Loneliness is not a well-trained dog that awaits our commands.

Like figs that grow when they are ready to grow and don't grow when they are not ready to grow, we have to await the proper conditions. We have to treat the soil and maximize the conditions for growth, but more than that we cannot do. We are not miracle workers. We are human beings.

Consider the suffering Jesus. He can tell us that what is guaranteed is the friendship of God in grief. What is not guaranteed is the absence of grief. It just comes. Grief and loneliness are around many corners for many people for much of the time. This is actually quite normal. Most people will gladly tell you how closely their real lives resemble the preposterous circumstances of soap operas or dramas. Only those of us who have neither observed nor experienced these things in our own lives will side with the farmer who wants the fig tree destroyed. Most of us would give it a little more time.

Chance things happen that are wonderful. Chance things happen that are horrible. Some fig trees yield fruit. Some don't. I can't grow sweet peas, but I've seen them flourishing in other people's gardens. We can't control everything. What we can do is continue to hope, we can fertilize things "one more year." And then we can wait on the Lord.

My Prayer...

O God, keep me willing to re-plant and re-fertilize until the time is right for growth. Don't let me count on myself too much. When loneliness comes to me, keep me from hating it or fearing it too much. I ask these things in the name of Jesus who didn't count so much on controlling life as loving it. Amen.

CHAPTER FIVE

Feeling All Alone

And the Spirit immediately drove him out into the wilderness. He was in the wilderness forty days, tempted by Satan; and he was with the wild beasts, and the angels waited on him (Mark 1:12).

I have just preached at my first church in honor of the 25th anniversary of my ordination to the Christian ministry. The text was the temptations of Jesus.

I was with my daughter and her friend in a motel in the foothills of Tucson, Arizona. The girls wanted to watch one more TV program before we went out to dinner. I was relegated to the side of the hill, outdoors, in the sweet February air.

I was deeply lonely when I got to that hill. First my husband wouldn't come on this trip. Then my sons refused. Then my daughter accepted, reluctantly, as long as she could bring a friend. Now, I couldn't even pull her from the television set. Poor me. My 25th anniversary, and here I was all alone.

And then the comic side of all this occurred to me. I began to laugh. Twenty-five years? Here I was alone on the side of the hill, looking over glittering Tucson, all before my very feet. And I thought again of Jesus' several temptations. "Power" as helping the poor, "power" as saving the city, "power" as stones becoming bread. I too have felt these temptations. I too have battled them.

Then I was shown where I really was. I was not above the city at all. All I had to do was turn and look up, and there in the foothills were the lights on in all the mountain houses. I was actually in the city, not looking over the city. I was not alone at all. I deeply thanked God that I was there in the midst of the people and not isolated by my ministry. Looking down at the city was part of my temptation. Again, I had responded eagerly to a mistaken interpretation.

After acknowledging how well I had dealt with all the temptations of my quarter decade, I felt a voice asking me, "Can we sign you up for another 25 years?" I said sure. As long as I'm not alone.

My Prayer...

Bless me, O God, and every one of us who has ever signed up for anything, so that we may keep our commitments, recognize our temptations, and then go on to find you, still our companion and still our friend. Turn our loneliness to solitude. Place us deep within your city and there let us rejoice. I ask in Jesus' name. Amen.

Chapter Six

The Weight of Things

They shall build up the ancient ruins; they shall raise up the former devastations; they shall repair the ruined cities, the devastations of many generations (Isaiah 61:4).

At the library, I came across *Fences, Borders, and Bridges: A Practical Manual,* a 1887 farming manual. It showed how to build a stone wall. "Never think of rock as too heavy," the manual advised. "Weight is its prime virtue."

It seems to me that loneliness is something like a rock. It feels heavy but when we know that weight may be its primary virtue, we will learn how to carry it.

Most people come to church from what they refer to erroneously as the "real world." There we purport to live between one version of heavy and another version of heavy, between a rock and a hard place. We come to church thinking we can get away from it all, only to find more of the same. But when we learn to value the burdens we carry, they don't seem so strange.

The opposite happens too. People see life as an oscillating set of difficulties, a load of heavy rocks. Our attitude about reality often makes reality what it is. Some people look at the massive challenges of the moment and declare spiritual bankruptcy. Others look at the same challenges and look for God. Still others see these difficulties and look to each other for help, for community, for comfort. Weight, they say, as old institutional boulders break apart, is the primary virtue of rocks and hard places. Weight is both a difficulty and a virtue for communities, too.

The ancient title of the Isaiah 61 text used above is a "psalm of deliverance to Zion." It reassures and encourages the people to rebuild, to raise up, to repair. Fallen stones can be rebuilt. They can make a new city. Ashes can be exchanged for a garland.

The promise of Isaiah, confirmed by Jesus, is that we don't have to carry so much around. We can exchange the spirit of heaviness for a garment of praise. We can live by a different set of guarantees. We can live knowing that we will be delivered. And we don't have to be afraid. We can move toward one another. We can realize that each of us is a little afraid, and a little lonely.

We can experience solitude even when we are not alone. It does come to those who take the time to nourish it, but it also comes for those who take the time to be together. Solitude is the act of being oneself with another. Our real self. To live as a Christian in these times is to live more deeply than the world lives. It is to live with our "rocks," not against them. It is to trust other people, to trust Jesus. It is no accident that Scripture says that Jesus "rolled away the stone."

But back to my little 1887 manual. It makes several suggestions about how to move the rocks for a wall. One is to throw a party. Get your friends in and make a challenge out of it. Good advice for the spiritual life too! The suggestion is to have strategic equipment, to build levers. Spiritual awareness is leverage. Very few of us have a spiritual strategy. We have strategies to retire or to get ahead in life, but not a spiritual strategy. By what guarantees do we want to live? Whose promise of deliverance do we believe?

These questions are a necessary part of both loneliness and solitude. The lack of a spiritual strategy is what keeps us lonely. We become disconnected one from another.

When we connect, God works through our connections to restore us and to make us less afraid. When we are restored, and when we become less afraid, we will discover solitude.

My Prayer...

O God, when I want to leave your world and become a world unto myself, draw me back to the promises of a better city. And let me be part of building it. Give me the gift of discovering my real self in community and let me give that gift to others as well. Amen.

CHAPTER SEVEN

Spiritual Rock Gardens

To provide for those who mourn in Zion...to give them a garland instead of ashes, the oil of gladness instead of mourning, the mantle of praise instead of a faint spirit (Isaiah 61:3).

*M*ost of the ugliness of the real world today is that nobody steps aside from it long enough to assess it. We are all feeding at the trough for too long much of our time. It is almost as though we are so afraid of loneliness that we never set ourselves on the road to solitude. Yet we pretty much have to be by ourselves to enjoy solitude. We need to accept the moments of loneliness that come with our solitude. There will always be moments of each.

We can be lonely in a big room. And we can know solitude at a huge banquet table. Loneliness becomes solitude when we turn off the radio and turn on our inner song.

Let me go back for a moment to my little manual about moving stone. It mentions a third way to move stone, which is not to move it at all, but rather to build around it. The manual says that the best place to begin a border is where the biggest stone already is. Rock gardeners say the same thing. They say that the best place to site a rock garden is the most difficult place, the least likely place. It is the same way the best architects design a house. They find a place and build around it. They let the land tell them what to do. We too have to let the physical and emotional terrain guide us. Though we live in difficult times, perhaps they will be the very best of times for us in the end precisely because they are so challenging. We have a chance to build a particularly beautiful spiritual house. Bounded by an abundance of rocks and hard places, our spiritual gardens have great possibilities for beauty.

Imagine what would happen if we took better care of our rocks and our hard places. Imagine what we might become. Imagine the strength we would acquire if we feared our loneliness less and were capable of moving closer to our own deepest fears. We would learn to become strong, strong like rock. So let's exchange our ashes for garlands, our mourning for the oil of gladness, and our faint spirits for mantles of praise.

My Prayer...

O God, sometimes I fear that "heaviness" is all there is. Put a garland instead of ashes around my neck. Anoint me with the oil of gladness and take away my mourning. Show me how to work with others, to share my loneliness, to value my solitude, and so begin again to rebuild my spiritual house. Amen.

CHAPTER EIGHT

Needing Friends

For it is a faithful saying that if we die with the Lord, we will also live with him (2 Timothy 2:11).

Oddly enough, a funeral can be as much a time for camaraderie as a time for sadness. At funerals, we can either enjoy great solitude or suffer great loneliness.

I write this from the hotel where I am staying for the funeral of one of my closest and oldest friends and mentors. She was present at every important moment of my life. All the old gang will gather, and I am eager to see them, but I have been crying for days. Some of my tears are because my friend has died too young. Some are for the sheer and utter loneliness of having to go on without her. And some of the tears are for all that we were not able to be for each other, that I was not able to walk in her shoes as I could have, might have.

If my friend had lived and it was I being buried, she might have felt the same. Yet, I would hope that she would not take all the blame. Even our most beloved dead may or may not have been the kind of friend others needed. But she would have understood, I hope, that not only the good parts of people die; they take their incompleteness along, too. Knowing one another's faults, however, doesn't make our grief and loss any less real.

The writer of second Timothy knows about the best kind of friendship, friendship with Jesus. About this he writes, "If we die with him, we also live with him. If we live with him, we also die with him." In a similar vein, a contemporary writer says that we live with those we die with. We die a little with those we live with.

It is said that H.L. Mencken put an envelope in a file that he knew would only be opened by the reporter who wrote his obituary. It contained only one line, "Don't overdo it." He knew that he had faults and weaknesses as well as talents, so it was important to him not to be inflated—even in death. To me, the best funeral would have plenty of tears and a very understated eulogy, one that alluded to the vices as well as the virtues of the deceased.

When all is said and done, the more we truly know one another, the less lonely we will be. The harder we work to really know one another, the less lonely we will be. We need friends—to know and to be known by, to live with and to die with.

My Prayer...

God, give me the grace to love my friends in spite of their faults, and to love myself in spite of my faults. Let me truly know others as they are. And grant that I might "live and die" with those around me, as fully as your Son lived and died with his disciples. Amen.

CHAPTER NINE

Nothing Is Perfect

❋

"Those who abide in me and I in them bear much fruit..." (John
15:5).

My daughter and I were walking through
Chinatown in San Francisco one gusty June
morning. Katie was just ten and not too knowl-
edgeable about either Chinatown or death. Along came a
funeral!

A brass band introduced the dozen limousines. In the
center of the procession was an open limo in which two
men bore a photo of their father, the deceased. It was
large, but not too large, just right for friends and acquain-
tances to recognize this man and his life. The sons held
the picture high. This man's death was an unlikely visita-
tion that day when we were looking for T-shirts. For his
family and friends it was equally unlikely that we would
witness their procession.

Katie looked at me perplexed. "They die in
Chinatown?" I could only reply with the obvious, "Yes,

22

I'm afraid they do."

These people were marking a father's passing with a ritual that made sense to them—though not to us. It occurred to me at that moment that our rituals help us to make it through the death of our loved ones. Even if they don't work for others, they work for us. They help us get through.

I personally want "My Lord, What a Morning" sung at my funeral. My husband thinks I'm nuts. He will have to decide whether my weird hope in the resurrection and the morning after will prevail over his own more muted way to mourn. We don't have to agree with our loved ones about what we want at our funeral, just as we don't have to like the way the Chinese tend their dead. But we do have to tend to one another, imperfections and all, while we're still on this journey.

There is, of course, no such thing as perfect "tending," save that done by Jesus. He keeps his end perfectly. We probably don't keep ours as well. The weeds in our gardens, to return to that metaphor, remind us that we are not perfect tenders. They demonstrate over and over that all growing comes from God. In our friendships, as in our gardens, there are weeds and thus there is always work to be done. But if we abide in Jesus, we will bear fruit, despite our own feeble efforts.

My Prayer...

Help me to tend those I love, O God, even you, especially you. Don't let me take you for granted and don't let me take my loved ones for granted. Keep me open to the goodness in others as well as the weaknesses. Thank you for the fruit I bear because of Jesus. Amen.

CHAPTER TEN

From the Inside Out

No good tree bears bad fruit, nor again does a bad tree bear good fruit; for each tree is known by its own fruit (Luke 6:43,44).

The trouble with most of us is that we have neglected to cultivate reflective interior lives. We buy, use, pollute, endanger and we do all this mindlessly. Our choices are influenced by outside forces, not from a deep spiritual life within.

I know one man who has come to a deep understanding of this problem. His name is John McNight. He has made a pilgrimage out of the world of criticism into the world of affirmation. He refuses to let the outside world enter and harm his inner life.

In his book *Building Communities from the Inside Out* (written with John Kretzmann), he outlines a new politics. He believes that a "needs mentality" has blinded us to the true assets of community. We have what we need! We just don't see ourselves that way. The book has been wildly popular, involving John in "thirty or forty calls per week," which, "ironically, invite the expert in to tell people that they don't need experts."

John accuses the media of "every night telling us that what we don't have is what is important." He says that even public agencies who assist the "needy" have fallen prey to this kind of thinking. They challenge people to give money even before determining the real needs of the people. In fact, "need" is not the only characteristic of our cities and towns. Real people live there. There are kids who know how to whistle and old people who have meditated long enough to know how to solve problems that others wouldn't dare tackle. Perhaps you have heard of the group of Salvadorans in North Carolina who created a soccer league to keep their community together; from its joy, came a church. Next a political movement. People do know how to build community!

McNight goes on to say that labels are "names for the emptiness some people see in other people." One effect of these labels is that they keep many community people from seeing the gifts of people who have been labeled. The label often blinds us to the capacity of the people who are named. Is the glass half full or half empty? McNight sees fullness and teaches others how to do the same. In a word, he is advancing solitude and the cultivation of it.

How can we begin to see our world from the inside out? How can we be good trees who bear much fruit? Only from deep within, only when we have solitude.

My Prayer...

O God, you created the world from your own inner joy. Help me to see and value it as you do. Help me to be a tree who bears good fruit that I might truly reach out to others. Help me to see clearly what is going on in the world. Amen.

Chapter Eleven

The Heavy Becomes Light

"For my yoke is easy and my burden is light" (Matthew 11:30).

Have you ever felt like you were carrying too much? I have. The weight of my burdens is often great. Sometimes I even see the people I love as burdens. I carry them. This carrying is complex and often is the cause of my loneliness. I put too many people into my life so I won't be lonely, and then I become lonely because there are too many people in my life.

Mostly the reason is that I feel I should protect people, especially my children. But how do we protect our children? How do we carry others without harming them or harming ourselves? How and when do we learn that the "yoke is easy and the burden is light"?

Do you remember Jessica, the little girl who died in a plane crash at age seven? She was with her father but she was flying the plane. Her parents let her do what seven-year-olds can't do. All of us feel the grip of parental irony.

We should not let them go. We must let them go. Frankly, we can do very little right. We can "over" parent and be in trouble—and we can "under" parent and be in trouble. We get lonely in these internal conversations with ourselves. We begin to feel heavy with the burden of caring for our children.

I remember once standing at the 30th Street train station in Philadelphia with my seven-year-old daughter. She handed me the gum she had been chewing and asked me to hold it. Excuse me, please, hold your own gum! But Mom, I thought you'd like to hold it. You don't want me to drop it on the ground, do you? Some mothers can't let their children let go of their childhood. Others rush them forward into responsibility (including handling their own gum).

My friend came up with a fairly decent solution to the standard enigma. Her 17-year-old daughter announced that she, like her two older brothers, would be hitchhiking across the country the summer after her senior year. Here was a wad of gum to hold! Both mother and father said she could not go. They wanted to keep their daughter safe and well.

The girl had none of it and she remade her announcement, only this time with the tears of fury and accusation. Her parents were sexist! My friend, that "sexist," overprotective mother, invited herself along on the trip the next morning. They both hitchhiked across the country that summer and had a great time (though they were nearly raped once).

What can parents do right? We can hold gum. We can refuse to hold gum. We can let our children fly. We can prohibit them from flying. We can also pray for them and for ourselves. It's amazing how few parents pray for themselves.

In my own way, I pray for myself more often now. It is the best thing I do for my solitude. I pray for safety, but also for the courage to take risks and to let my children take risks.

Even our children are not our children. They need to have their own adventures so they can get to their own solitude. We must care for them as Christ cares for us— freely, openly, without control, daring us to fly, sometimes long before we are ready.

My Prayer...

God of the easy yoke, there are so many things I can do wrong. I have done most of them already and will do them again tomorrow. But come and remind me of how you love me. keep me safe—and keep me ready for adventure too—and let me do the same for those I love. Amen.

CHAPTER TWELVE

Time for God

Remember the Sabbath day and keep it holy (Exodus 20:8).

One of the reasons we are as lonely as we are is that we have forgotten to keep the Sabbath. We don't separate our time into solitude and community, time and eternity, us and God. We don't "go away" even when we take trips. We stay plugged in to external forces—and we become exhausted and apart.

Many of my friends say they'd love to see me—if they could stand seeing anyone. I feel exactly that way about them.

Whatever happened to Sabbath? It was the day taken off from work for God and worship, and it was a time for rest, and yes, solitude. It was not a time for television and its dramatic replacement of our story with someone else's story. It was not a time for shopping, doing errands, or getting caught up on our desk stress as we pay our bills.

Sabbath is a time for God. Sabbath is religious rest. It is time for play, a pause from the routine of work.

Because of enormous changes in the way our week is structured, Sabbath has all but disappeared. Time for God is a luxury that even the richest people in the world don't enjoy. Because of the way contemporary work is structured, Sabbath is now a discipline we have to make and do ourselves. If we do not separate our own time, no one will do it for us.

In our middle-class American world today, we "work" most of the time. Work is anything we have to do; whereas "playing" is what we want to do. Most of us think we have obligations most of the time; there is no time for just being still, for reflecting, for prayer. We rush from one place to another. Time is a digital clock, where minutes matter. But Sabbath can be our connection to God and to solitude.

It's a shame that we have lost this time of rest because with it has gone our sense of the sacredness of time. And yet we let it happen to ourselves. This loss has made us terribly lonely: we are lonely for God. But we are not without hope. Restoration is something remarkably easy to do. We simply have to do less, not more.

Sometimes to fully enjoy our friends and families, we have to get away from them for a while. We have to go away to God. The return to friends and families will be good. We will then be who we want to be with them. Why? Because we have been with our God.

My Prayer...

Guard my going out and my coming in from this day forward, O God. May I become once again a Sabbath person who takes time to connect with you and with my inner life. And then may I share the gifts of my solitude with those I love. Amen.

CHAPTER THIRTEEN

The Place of Prayer

And he spoke a parable to them, that all ought always to pray, and not to be fainthearted... (Luke 18:1).

As Christians, we know we are a part of one another and that we should hold all things in common. We know that we should pray. We know that we should spend time alone but also together, and that we should do all of these things well. But instead, we are fainthearted. We are not all that we want to be and there just doesn't seem to be time enough to become what we know we ought to be.

Lack of time seems like such an excellent excuse for not balancing our need for solitude with our need for community. Yet, we all know that it is not really the reason for our failure and our faintheartedness. We have simply lost touch with what is most important, and we have thus become deeply lonely. How then does this conflict get resolved? First of all, we have to be aware that there is a conflict, and we have to pray for guidance. Prayer is the ultimate solution.

Think about it. What counts most in life is love, love for God and love for one another. That's all there is. But when we believe in these two, we are in fairly constant conflict with our own culture. Our culture says that self-fulfillment and self-concern are first and foremost. This self absorption alienates us from God and one another.

Modern families gives witness to this. Family members no longer eat together, play together, talk together, or pray together. They are isolated from one another. They are lonely and don't know why. A pastor in a small hill town said to me recently, "I don't think I could face the daily stress my fifteen-year-old faces." How much stress could there be in a small town, I wondered. But then it dawned on me that she faces the same amount as teenagers in big cities because the stress is the result of a surplus of stimulation.

The average person today experiences fifteen times the stimulation as people in a previous era. Children multiply this stimulation by the kinds of games they play and television shows they watch. The loss that results from excess stimulation is the loss of sacred time, "enchanted" time. Prayer is this enchanted, sacred time. Sacred time restores us to our solitude, which restores our capacity to be a community of love. Prayer is not for the fainthearted!

My Prayer...

Keep me, O God, faithful to the practice of prayer, alone and with my family. Help me to be centered on what is important: love for you and love for others. May I learn to balance my need for solitude with my need for community and may I never be fainthearted about seeking it. Amen.

CHAPTER FOURTEEN

We Need Time Alone

After Jesus read from the scroll of Isaiah, about the spirit of the Lord being upon him to proclaim good news to the poor, the people were filled with rage. They got up and led him to the brow of the hill, intending to hurl him off the cliff. But he passed through their midst and went on his way (Luke 4:28–30).

Why do we need time alone? For starters, time alone teaches us to bother, to notice, to see, and to care. These are religious motions and emotions. If we do not make these moves or feel these things, the capacity for them dies in us. If we are not able to move and be moved religiously, we die spiritually. In the Scripture cited above, Jesus made a big announcement about taking care of the poor and the city and the people. When his listeners became angry, he disappeared and went on his way to a time of solitude and prayer.

We need to do the same, especially if we are struggling to bring others to spiritual rebirth. We may need even more time alone, not less, if we are to make a difference in today's spiritually dead culture. From deep within our solitude and apartness, there are things we can do. We can more deeply take notice of what is going on. Too often our "activism" keeps us from noticing.

We can, for example, notice the closing of a hospital or the move of a factory. Within the solitude that we share with God, we can pray for the people whose lives are affected. We can bother, notice, see, lament, care. We can do all these things and many more once we have taken the time to be apart with God.

We can take a hint from Jesus, who clearly had more capacity for action than most of us do and who clearly spent more time in solitude with God than most of us do.

Many of you may have had a childhood like mine. It was marked by anxiety about jobs. My father took a low-rung management job and did not join the Garment Workers Union because "I want you to have a college education." He worked thirty years in dedicated service to a company that ran south in the fifties. We moved every year for his company from the time I was eleven until I was eighteen. His final layoff, after several earlier ones, was at age sixty—without a pension.

People all around us today are experiencing similar losses. Is there a way we can learn to hear and to care? Jesus points the way: go into the desert—or to your own place of solitude—and experience God's love and guidance. We will then begin to notice the trouble and the hurt. God will fill us with what we need when we return from our apartness.

My Prayer...

Help me to find a place where I can be alone with you, O God. There let me notice what is going on through your eyes. When I return to my community, strengthen me to act in your name to make this world a better place. Amen.

CHAPTER FIFTEEN

Time Together

All who believed were together and had all things in common. They would sell their possessions and goods and distribute the proceeds to all, as any had need... They ate their food with glad and generous hearts, praising God (Acts 2:44–46).

There really is no such thing as a private person. Solitude, while deeply desirable for many reasons, exists on behalf of God and community and depth of self. It is not an end in itself. Solitude does not mean that we isolate ourselves—but that we more deeply connect.

I have a good friend who swears he is a self-made man. I always have to remind him that he inherited his insurance agency from his father! He denies his connection to his father at great peril to himself. It will isolate him over time. He will begin to believe his own press releases.

We believe in the myth of the private person at our own peril. The very myth isolates us profoundly. It moves us to reside in a world that doesn't really exist—but because we think it does, we keep trying to make it on our own. We imagine an isolated world where we are supposed to get our own jobs, raise our own kids, drive our own car (even pay fines to drive it solo in the fast lanes normally reserved for multi-passenger vehicles). There is an alternative to the myth of individualism. It is the deep knowledge that we are part one of another.

I recently met one of the pastors of a large African-American church. She told me a very moving story about how Little Flower, a local orphanage, dropped off a van full of girls at the church one Saturday afternoon. The girls said, "We were told you could teach us to dance." Somehow the rumor had gone out that the church was holding dancing classes. It was not. But those girls got a dancing lesson on the spot.

This is a "mega church"; it does a little of everything for over 5000 people a week. How do they do it? By firmly "living" the belief that we are part one of another, that we hold all things, even our time, in common.

No, I don't think that we should hold dancing classes on the spot for everyone who shows up. But we should face the truth that we are not on our own; we are part of a community. Togetherness can be an awful burden at times. But it is also a marvelous joy. Imagine the day when all the people in the world will "eat their food with glad and generous hearts, praising God." I long for the day when this will happen again.

My Prayer...

Lord, give me the courage to accept the truth about myself. I am not alone, but part of a community. You once said that it was not good for man or woman to be alone. Keep me from the dangerous myth of individualism that I may know you and others as you want me to. Amen.

CHAPTER SIXTEEN

Feeling Powerless

There was a certain rich man, who was clothed in fine purple and fine linen, and he ate sumptuously every day. And there was a certain beggar named Lazarus, who laid at the rich man's gate, full of sores (Luke 16:19,20).

One of the loneliest feelings I have ever known has to do with the poor, with people like the beggar Lazarus. It came after reaching as far as I've known how for them and not being able to "touch" them. At times like this, I am reminded of Toni Morrison's distinction between a spectacle and a ritual. One tells the truth, the other acts it out.

I have already made a "spectacle" of myself in trying to change a world that won't budge. I have worked in soup kitchens, and founded soup kitchens, and wiped blood off the floors of soup kitchens, after guests drew knives on each other. These were, after all, only ritual feedings, though I wanted them to be more than that. They did not change the power balance between the rich man and Lazarus.

The times I have been most deeply alone in my life are

times when I have had to admit my failure to change this. Lazarus' sores remain open. I have stepped over the bodies of women in Grand Central Station, women whose pants had holes in them, whose ragged underwear showed through, whose dirty fingernails made me queasy. That was only on one night, one late train, but figuratively speaking, I lift my feet daily over Lazarus at the gate.

Vaclav Havel speaks of the power of powerlessness being the salvation of his people. I know what he means. I want to believe that my drops in the bucket mean something. And power comes through this truth. Just as it came from Jesus who tells us that the little means a lot. He and we and God must form a cooperative. My little drop is my piece. Your little drop is your piece. Thus do the loaves and fishes multiply. God receives these offerings and multiplies them into a grand feast.

What breaks me out of my yearning to touch the poor, my lonely desperation for justice, is confidence that God can work the small into the large, the lonely into the connected. God can most surely do what I cannot.

My Prayer...

Oh God, be with me in my deep and powerless loneliness regarding the poor. Keep me from being too much like the rich man. Help me to believe that all of your Lazaruses can be fed. Multiply my loaves and fishes and make of them a feast. Amen.

CHAPTER SEVENTEEN

We Are Not God

Everyone who strives for mastery is temperate in all things. I therefore so run, so fight, not as one who beats the air... (1 Corinthians 9:25–27).

*P*aul runs and fights but is temperate in the way he does it. He doesn't beat more air than is necessary! He suggests that we do have great mastery and great capacity, but we are not gods. Often the source of our loneliness and isolation is the false assumption that we are God or gods ourselves.

Those of us who are striving for mastery still need God's guidance. Otherwise, we will fail at even the little good we might have done for others. We will become exactly the lonely people we are so desperate not to become. We will reach out, but not touch other lives.

Paul understands that he is not God. I am not "one who beats the air." When we think we are God, we think we can do everything, be everything, go anywhere.

Airplanes are a good metaphor for mastery and for the

limits of our mastery. We love our airplanes because they have conquered the skies and taken us where we could never go before. But we fear them, too, because they can harm us, even kill us. We don't want to rely on them without reservation. We don't want to burn our wings—as Icarus did—by flying too close to the sun. We don't want to overstep our limits.

When we begin to understand our limits (and the limits of our magnificent technology), we begin to say yes to them. When we say yes to our limits, we are not afraid to be just what we are. Our mastery, of course, comes from God. God came among us. Why? To keep us from being alone in our fear.

My Prayer...

Let me not be afraid of my power and mastery so much, O God, as I am afraid of misusing it. Direct my abilities to your ends, and let me fly in unconceited ways. Give me a right size, a human size, and let me be content with what I am. I ask this in the name of Jesus who came among us. Amen.

CHAPTER EIGHTEEN

Hungry People

❋

I am the bread of life. Whoever comes to me will never be hungry (John 6:35).

We are hungry people. We have more than any people in the entire world, and yet we are starving. What do we say we want? We want time. We want peace. We have them but we don't know it. We are lonely for time and peace. We might say we are lonely for God.

People say that what they want from church is something to take home, something good that lasts, food that feeds and nourishes. There are many obstacles in our way to this kind of food, however. The biggest one is our addiction to activity and noise, our bad habit of tuning God out. Habits run very deep, even religious habits. St. Paul says it this way: "the good that I want to do, I don't do, and the evil that I don't want to do, I do!" We eat "junk food" instead of the spiritual food that leads us to God. Like any addiction, this addiction to the junk food of noise and activity is hard to overcome.

But we can take a first step with God's help. On this
very day, find a quiet place and sit there for a while. Read
a passage from Scripture. Talk to God simply and freely.
To do these things, we have to turn off the TV, put away
the newspaper, resist the urge to jump up and do something.

What we really hunger for is the bread of life. We are
actually starving for it. And yet, our contemporary experience is hunger. In this best fed, "all you can eat" country, we are hungry. So what is the Christian answer with
regard to hunger? "I am the bread of life…whoever comes
to me will not hunger and will not thirst." Eucharist, yes.
God, yes. Let's eat!

My Prayer…

*God, O God, thank you for the time and space known as Sabbath
in which good food will come to us, even the bread of life. We know
you stand ready to feed us in a great banquet. Let us partake of it
and you, today and forever. Amen.*

CHAPTER NINETEEN

Far Away from Home

For God so loved the world... (John 3:16).

The loneliest I have ever been in "place" terms is when I attended the UN Conference for Women in Beijing. I was twelve hours out of my time zone. I was on the opposite side of the world from my children. I couldn't speak the language and I had been denied papers even to the Huairou Conference, which was already once removed from the city conference. The reason? I had innocently and stupidly put on my visa application the truth that I was a writer going to report on the conference.

And yet, my very lack of papers brought me into what were to be some of the great intimacies and solitudes of my life. Intimacy is the opposite of loneliness: we are met by an "other." Solitude is the other side of both intimacy and loneliness: we are met by our self. In Beijing, slogging through the rain of city streets, with all the women of the world an hour away, I met "myself" in small vegetable stands bargaining for peanuts, or in parks where old men took their birds out for a walk, or in the midst of older women practicing their Tai Chi who didn't mind my presence.

One of the women in my tour group died in Beijing, and so did her husband. They were in a car accident on the ride to Huairou. The tour leaders asked me to prepare a little "service" for the other 150 women in our group. I have never had to dig so deep for prayers.

Another woman in the group split her spleen. I visited her in the Beijing "western" hospital, which was filthy, crowded, and frightening. The Chinese hospitals are atrocious in every one of these respects, plus they use a medicine that is very un-Western in its healing powers. But western women, during the UN meeting, were all directed to this "western" style hospital.

The intimacy I developed with Jean, as she lay in the intensive care unit of this hospital, waiting for her husband to arrive from North Carolina, was astonishing. We spoke of life and death and love as if we had known each other our whole lives. When I accompanied her 75-year-old husband through the open corridors (when he arrived after a 72-hour trip, which his doctor had advised him against in the first place), he walked into the room and laughed for joy because she was still alive.

Even there, so far away, the spark that connects people couldn't be put out.

Chinese women were not allowed to attend the conference. But the eleven Chinese women who were assigned to the floor of my hotel got quite an education. Two were part of the soldier force on the 11th floor. With my permission, the other nine inspected my suitcases, computer equipment, and family photos. Two helped me connect my modem. Across language barriers, we could still establish ties of intimacy. Though I experienced loneliness in that faraway place, I also experienced solitude and solidarity. I felt connected.

My Prayer...

Take me out of the small world of my own loneliness and fear, O God, and place me where every woman and every man walks. Let me touch others in hospital corridors and on dirt roads. Wherever I am, please connect me to your Son, who is already with me, traveling at my side. Amen.

CHAPTER TWENTY

Dealing with Our Fears

Love your enemies; be good to those who hurt you (Matthew 5:44).

Sometimes when we are alone we wonder if we have anything inside us. Solitude knows a "self" and walks with him or her. But loneliness can't find an inner self. Very often it is fear that causes loneliness.

When we begin to fear, we are too absorbed and distracted to focus on God and thus we know the excruciating emptiness of loneliness. We wonder if there is anyone inside there, with us, out here, all alone. We become our own worst enemy.

Some of our enemies are outside, where we work perhaps or even where we worship. Surely Jesus was speaking of these enemies when he advised loving them. He meant a social love. And he may have meant something more, since some of our enemies are within. Fear leads the way, but there is also pride, revenge, and anger. Must we also love these enemies? In a sense, yes. These feelings are a part of who we are. By befriending them, lov-

ing them, holding them out to God, we diminish their
hold on us. When we forget about ourselves, we defeat
our internal enemies. We give our better self a chance to
work. We acknowledge both how wonderful and how
terrible we sometimes are. We become a friend to all of
our self.

Jesus applauded self-forgetfulness. "Letting go" is the
foundation of the capacity to love our enemies. We have
to let go of whatever it is we are protecting about ourselves and make room for the other. The Buddhist tour
guide in the movie, *Beyond Rangoon,* describes what ani-
mates Aung San Suu Kyi, Nobel prize winning activist in
Burma: "She is not watching herself."

We achieve our best selves by not watching ourselves,
by accepting ourselves. We achieve deep inner peace
then, otherwise known as solitude.

My Prayer...

*Give me a way, O God, to know myself well enough not to be afraid
of what is inside me. Help me not to watch myself, but instead to
watch you and listen to you. Then let me return to the world to love
and serve others as fully as I can. Amen.*

CHAPTER TWENTY-ONE

Fixing Broken Glass

The people who walked in darkness have seen a great light (Isaiah 9:2).

I was staying overnight with our pastor in North Adams. I needed some computer assistance the following morning. She took me to her neighbor and deacon, Bill Cummings, who is clearly the premier stained-glass repairman in the country. The certificates on his wall so demonstrate—but the light in his eye makes the point much more clearly.

He is repairing panels from the Vatican and from churches around the country, as well as assorted art works. There are several people employed in the minute repair of broken glass. The colors in the large barn studio dazzle, as do the broken panels. One man has been working for two years on a certain alabaster yellow!

The early morning light helped the scene to dazzle both my soul and my eyes. I found the quiet solitude of this working shop as moving as the light. The artists work long hours alone, fixing broken glass. They attend to the glass. They repair the light.

I "repair" broken churches for a living too. I should skip the spiritual autobiography and focus on the artist, the studio, the task, the magnificent morning solitude, but surely I am not the only one who is moved by the repair of broken glass. I have not put all my faith in plexiglass. I know that stones are being thrown at our beautiful windows, at the magnificent treasure of our faith. Our work is to restore the windows of our churches, to let the light shine.

It takes deep solitude to connect the inner energy required for this work. There will be times of loneliness, when we swear the glass cannot be repaired. We will fear that things are too shattered to ever be whole again. But then we will go back to work, believing that we will eventually see a great light.

My Prayer...

May those who walk in darkness and on broken glass have their eyes and their light restored, great God. Repair what is broken in me so that I may be whole. Let me see the light. Keep me from fear; restore my peace and calm. Amen.

CHAPTER TWENTY-TWO

Focusing on God

O Lord, our God, other Lords besides you have ruled over us, but we acknowledge your name alone (Isaiah 26:13).

In "Nighthawks," the great Hopper canvas, there is a lonely man with a cup of coffee, all by himself, though sitting in a public space. The canvas is narrowly but brilliantly staged, emptied of trivial details and subtly distorted for dramatic impact. Just the human being, just sitting at the diner's counter. There are a lot of other things in the picture but we don't see them. The light focuses us.

If we want to be focused, we can use the artist's example. We can learn to see what we need to see. We can paint our lives with the light. We can be alone, in public, at night. We can hawk the night.

Focus often comes in the solitude of a cup of coffee, in times apart, in times with self and with God. Focus comes when we look at only God and God alone, as Isaiah recommends in the Scripture passage above. We can screen out the other data.

A parish "street sweep" on the steps of the great Sacred Heart cathedral does just this. Every morning he sweeps up the broken wine bottles and empty potato chip bags off the steps. All day long the faithful go in and out of the cathedral. At night the revelers arrive. They leave a mess. I saw that street sweeper one morning when I went there at dawn. At one point, between steps, he leaned on his shaggy broom and closed his eyes. He prayed. He acknowledged only God. The rubble disappeared for a few comforting minutes.

What does solitude give us? It gives us time for God. It sweeps the rubble out of the picture. It keeps the picture focused and it keeps our spiritual life focused.

My Prayer...

O God, unclutter my life, please. Let me see only you. Let me use the light to find out what is important. Let me see all the way to you and learn your way for me. Amen.

CHAPTER TWENTY-THREE

Remembering Saves Us

But God remembered Noah and all the wild animals and all the domestic animals that were with him in the ark (Genesis 8:1).

Memory often saves us from loneliness. Let those who can, remember! Let us remember the way God remembered Noah, and Noah remembered God. Let us not forget one another.

A good friend of mine is losing his memory at age 65. I can only imagine his loneliness. He is noticing how much he forgets. It takes enormous courage to acknowledge our forgetfulness. And remembering not to forget puts us in a bit of a bind! Especially when forgetfulness is the problem in the first place.

I imagine a kind of prayer as being the solution to the problem. That we pray for God's guidance and then just accept what is going on neurologically as a new kind of brain, a new kind of home. It comes down to "letting go."

For those of us with minor forgetfulness, the same solution is necessary. We can pray for small memories, small openings on our past, small connections. They will become the thread we need to remember in the way God remembers. I have learned that God works in the cracks and crevices. I have learned to be wary of the big and the bogus. God remembered the animals two by two, and clearly God could have "remembered" them all.

Sometimes we are blocked by thinking of God's action as grand. Often it is not. It is sometimes a small crack in the door, and always one that lets us squeak through to freedom and the companionship of God. We need only remember the important thing, which is that we are not alone.

My Prayer...

Guard my memory, O God, as you guard me. Even if I forget everything else, let me remember that you are with me. You didn't abandon Noah, or the animals, and you won't abandon me, either. Amen.

CHAPTER TWENTY-FOUR

We Are All "Different"

❋

Man...(or woman) shall not live by bread alone (Luke 4:4).

There is more to life than bread. There is bread plus. No matter how alone we become, or how isolated we imagine we are, there is still more than bread, more than here and now, more than this moment of trouble. There is also, of course, more than us.

I think of some runners I saw once in a Special Olympics race. They looked ridiculous to the ablebodied people on the sidelines. But then I realized something important about myself. I too am disabled, handicapped, differently labeled—say it as you will. So are you.

A line from Anton Boisen centers me when I get afraid of not being enough. He said that human initiative is not the core of reality. Holiness is God at the core. God finds us. Our "ability" and capacity are not what really matters: what matters is the core of reality, which is God's ability and God's capacity.

There may be nothing we can do to change our loneliness or isolation. We may just have to sit there with it, or limp along with it, or run a funny race with it. God will come when God is ready to come to liberate us. We wait if we can in solitude, not in loneliness. Life is more than bread; it is more than our capacity or ability.

If Anton Boisen was right about anything, he was right about human initiative. Human initiative is not at the core. God is at the core. God will find you, and God will find me.

My Prayer...

When I imagine your world as smaller than it is, O God, remind me of its size. Remind me of your presence at the core of my existence. Startle me. Wake me up. Show me what is really going on, that I am not alone but that you are with me in my solitude, in my bread, and in all that I do and am. Amen.

CHAPTER TWENTY-FIVE

Trust Can Open Doors

Ask it shall be given you, Seek and you shall find. Knock and the doors will be open to you (Matthew 7:7).

*F*or all we know, the doors we imagine to be closed may be open even now. We may have become so attached to our moods and distractions that we haven't tried to open them.

When we begin to activate our faith again, to live as though God is active on our behalf, many things, formerly hazy, become clear. We test the doors. We trust the doors to open.

Last winter, when there was a great deal of snow, I was at the airport and overheard a traveler screaming at a TWA attendant: "But I have to get to New York tonight." "Oh, no, you don't," said the attendant.

The doors will open. We will get to New York when we get to New York. Then, we trust, the doors will open and let us out. God is always at work, even when our brains are not. And, as everyone knows, doors can open from the inside too. Trust is the way doors open.

My ten-year-old daughter locked herself in her room one Saturday afternoon, by total accident. The doorknob simply fell off the door. She stayed in there for two hours and sixteen minutes (but who was counting), and as she will be glad to tell you now, "did not cry." The only thing she worried about was what would happen if she had to go to the bathroom. Why didn't she cry? Quoting again, "Because I knew you would finally come home and let me out."

My Prayer...

I may be stuck, O God, but you are not. I may be locked up inside myself, in a compartment made small by my fear, but you are not bound. You are free. If I seek you, I can find you. You will open the door, one way or the other. Teach me how to trust in you. Amen.

CHAPTER TWENTY-SIX

Take Nothing for the Journey

❈

He ordered them to take nothing for their journey except a staff; no bread, no bag, no money in their belts, but to wear sandals and not to put on two tunics (Mark 6:8–9).

What worries me? My weight. There is more of me than there should be. What else worries me? My fights with old friends over politics, and making new friends even when I don't keep up with the old. I also worry about my greed for life, which is a great blessing and a great curse. I worry too about having so many possessions when others have so little. I am afraid that I make a lousy disciple. There is too much of me and my worries to carry around.

Yielding to these worries makes me feel very lonely. Ironically, much of my loneliness comes to me by way of these worries. I go deep inside. I forget to talk to others about just how silly some of my concerns are. I forget to talk to God. In many ways we are all the same, both very full and very busy, and very empty and very worried. Our loneliness comes from this strange mix which is simultaneously "too much and too little."

Jesus says to carry only a pair of sandals and a tunic, and I think, "My God, how would we ever manage?" But every now and then I see beyond my possessions and my worry, and I understand what Jesus means. My life is cluttered, and I don't trust that God will provide. I understand a smidgen of what Jesus was saying to his disciples about "taking" nothing for their journey. If I let go of what I don't need, double portion returns to me. I hear Gandhi's gifted words, "Don't want what others can't have."

Being needy inside the experience of "too much" is standard American fare. We have it all, but we are still needy and lonely. When we share our experiences with one another, we at least help with the loneliness.

I like to think that God has a great city in mind for the whole world. In that city, we all will dance wearing sandals. We need take nothing for this journey. We will be full. We will not be lonely any more.

My Prayer...

O God, with deep thanksgiving for the fullness you offer, I rest now in your care, hoping that my greed for even good things will not prevent me from knowing you and your intentions for my life. Let me dance with a light heart and a full heart. Amen.

CHAPTER TWENTY-SEVEN

Sharing Holy Food

After blessing the bread, he broke it and gave it to them saying, "Take: this is my body, broken for you." Then he took a cup...and all of them drank from it (Mark 14:22–23).

A very poor woman I once knew had three children. Many nights she served them pork and beans, but they ate at a table with a linen table cloth (tattered though it was). She knew that sharing food, no matter how simple, was a holy action. Unfortunately, many of us today rush through our meals, the cooking as well as the eating.

Even in our churches people complain that communion takes too long. This attitude towards eucharist tells all. It says that we worship time more than the holy one who is at table with us. This is the real reason that many of our liturgies are more often spectacles than worship. We only pretend to worship God.

Eucharist is an act of great personal faith as well as one of the most communal things we do. Can we be lonely at

God's table? I think not, especially if we slow down long enough to remember who and whose we are.

Major religions have always linked food and faith. Bernard Glassman in *Instructions to the Cook: a Zen Master's Lessons in Living a Life that Matters* (Bell Tower, 1996), encourages us to eat consciously and well. Last year he held a Passover Seder for homeless men in New York City's Bowery district. He sees Zen as nothing more or less than the art of eating a good meal. In a good meal, we throw nothing away; we use what we have. Even the faults we bring with us to the table are part of the ingredients.

In spite of all the food available to us, our contemporary experience is of hunger. Eucharist means fullness of soul and fullness of belonging. Eucharist is the best food in the world. It puts us at table with God and with one another, and in this bread and cup we find abundance. The "little" is plenty. We become full instead of "eucharistically starving," as Rosemary Radford Ruether puts it.

We are no longer alone; we are fed and accompanied by the body of Christ.

My Prayer...

I am hungry O God, hungry for you. Please feed me with the Bread of Life that I might share it with those around me who are also hungry for you. In deep solitude that marvels in the beauty of your holy food, I pray. Amen.

CHAPTER TWENTY-EIGHT

A Salute to Stillness

Be still and know that I am God (Psalm 46:10).

On Good Friday, Jesus experienced the ultimate loneliness, abandonment on the cross. But I really believe that he also experienced the greatest solitude. It is good for us to be "still" with him, to look at our broken places in his presence. We can stand with him at the cross and both weep and rejoice.

I often use the line of Scripture cited above to calm myself down. It reminds me of what I already know. It helps me to just "be" in God's presence, to live in the present moment. How was Jesus able to endure that sense of abandonment? No doubt he was able to turn his loneliness into solitude through acceptance. And his acceptance came because of his oneness with God and God's plan for him. Jesus had hope that there would be an Easter Sunday.

Paul Tillich says in his sermon "The Right to Hope" that hope is like a seed or a womb. What is needed is preexistent. We bring the hope with us, unborn. "In the seed of a tree, stem and leaves are already present, and this gives us the right to sow the seed in hope for the fruit. We have no assurance that it will develop." But Jesus hoped in God's promise, and it was fulfilled. And we are his followers.

My Prayer...

O God, may I, too, have the gift of hope. May I believe in your promises and listen to you in stillness. May I experience true solitude, the kind that Jesus knew. Amen.

CHAPTER TWENTY-NINE

Living Our Own Lives

Has the Lord spoken only through Moses? Has he not spoken through us also? (Numbers 12:2).

Aaron and Miriam are jealous of Moses. They couldn't see the beauty of their own revelations; they wanted to be Moses, instead of being Aaron and Miriam.

They acted out of their loneliness, not their solitude. Loneliness leads to greed; it spends a lot of time wanting what other people have and neglecting what is already given. We refuse what is on our plate because we want what is on someone else's plate. What is astonishing is that the "someone else" probably wants what we have.

This covetousness creates incredible loneliness. It pushes us deep inside in a negative way. Solitude, on the other hand, drives us deep inside in a positive way. What is the secret to solitude? I believe the secret is taking time to be thankful for our own revelation and leaving other people's revelations to them.

The Benedictines wash dishes with feeling. The Zen Buddhists clean the kitchen before they cook and after they cook. Why? Because cleaning the kitchen clears the mind. It is marvelous how rested a clear mind is—and how tired a cluttered one is. If Zen Buddhists can do one thing at a time, and Benedictines can do one thing at a time, so can we. We can live our lives, not someone else's life.

The Vietnamese Zen thinker Thich Nhat Hahn puts it this way: "While washing the dishes, you might be thinking about the tea afterwards, and so try to get them out of the way as quickly as possible in order to sit and drink tea. But that means that you are incapable of living during the time you are washing dishes."

Rollo May in *The Awakened Heart* declares that our spiritual home is always right where we are. He teaches us to be delighted in our own portion and to be less jealous of the portion of others. May wants us to be at home at home and at home at work. "When you are there (here), stretch and yield lovingly into the real-life activity of now. Try a little consecrated Zen. Do one thing at a time, with complete immediate mindfulness. Don't do it to get it done so you can get on to the next thing. Do it for love. Do it now. *Then* do the next thing." May says that he knows that life can be lived this way because he does live this way, as he puts it, four or five minutes a day. I appreciate his humility.

Even though I am writing this, even though I know that doing one thing at a time is the right way to live, I will soon be back to my usual life, robbing Peter to pay Paul, missing too much of Jacob's soccer game because of a work appointment, missing too much of a work appointment to go to Katie's soccer game. I am trying to succeed at living too much and living too well, a particularly modern form of sin.

Why can I not be what I am? Because I haven't connected my loneliness to my solitude, that's why. I haven't made the connection between my greed and my gratitude, and both live deep within me.

My Prayer...

O God, help me to be here with you as I pray, not off somewhere making plans or dreaming false dreams. Help me to recognize the revelations you give me and to proclaim your presence in all that I do. Amen.

CHAPTER THIRTY

Friends with Jesus

"But I have called you friends" (John 15:15).

*F*riendship is the opposite of being alone, but real friendship is as rare as it is precious. Genuine friendship comes with, not against, genuine solitude. Once we can manage joyfully by ourselves, we can usually find a friend. Native Americans tell us not to destroy the "seed" corn. Jesus is like the seed corn of our best selves, and he has called us friends. Friends help us protect our innermost seed. Friendship transcends our loneliness because a true friend sees all of us and accepts us as we are.

Yet we dare not let our hope hang on our sleeve. When we walk into a room, we look for our own. We don't look for our opposites. But we do hope for a world where friendship might be possible with those who think their own thoughts and not just ours.

What makes us lonely in the first place? The root is not the absence of friends. Often we are lonely with our friends as well as lonely for want of them. Loneliness has deep roots. It can be the unconscious fear that there is no hope for friendship across racial or economic lines. Can I be friends with an illiterate person? Can she dare friendship with me? Yes, in the friendship of Jesus.

When Jesus says that we are his friends, he does not mean the friendship of equals and the like-minded. He means the friendship of abundant love, where we need not be equal to receive it. He means the friendship of God and human, in which we humans are drawn deep to our inner seed. In this friendship, more is possible than when the seed is buried, or unwatered, or sown in bad ground. In this kind of friendship, more is possible than we have ever imagined.

My Prayer...

O God, you make all things new and more possible than I ever imagined. Grant me genuine friendship with you so that I may yet come to know what your son described as friendship with him. Protect me from loneliness and fear. Amen.

CHAPTER THIRTY-ONE

God's Beautiful Sculpture

"Love your neighbor as you love yourself" (Matthew 19:19).

My son said it was "embarrassing" to write about himself. I told him that writing an essay about yourself is like looking at a beautiful sculpture. What part of that is you? What part of humanity are you?

In some ways it's easier to love our neighbor than to love ourselves. There is a presumption, especially among women, that we should always come "last." That is not what the golden rule says or means: it means that self and neighbor are both part of the whole. We should love our neighbors as ourselves.

I loved the line describing Katharine White in a recent *New Yorker* issue, all about and by women. White was a genuine self. William Maxwell said, "It's funny as an editor, she was maternal, and as a mother, she was editorial." The author Nancy Franklin did not miss the conundrum of the comment. "Men tend to see their lives, regardless of the balance of the various parts, as a unified whole, but the prevailing metaphor for women...has failure built into it: we are said to "juggle" the various parts of our lives, and the only possible outcome if we concentrate on one ball in particular is that we drop the others. But this is not how Katharine White saw her life—partly because she could afford not to, by hiring people to juggle for her, but mainly because she just didn't think that way. When I started looking at her life as she looked at it—and as she lived it—it suddenly seemed all of a piece."

I recently spent the weekend reading Louise Bogan's biography, *Journey Around My Room,* and in it she says "the certain method of stilling poetic talent is to substitute an outer battle for an inner one. A poet emerges from a spiritual crisis strengthened and refreshed only if s/he has been strong enough to fight it through at all levels, and at the deepest first. One refusal to take up the gage thrown down by his/her own nature leaves the artist confused and maimed...."

We become a self by connecting our inner and outer self. In becoming a self, we write our own "poem." We mature into selves. We put away the myths others have of us. We can then connect deeply with one another, not just as a way out of loneliness, but more as a way of obeying the golden rule.

But how do we become "selves" when so much of the world is encouraging us to become things? It's a constant struggle. We desperately want to become ourselves and we want this for our children too. I personally want to see myself in that beautiful sculpture and I want my son to see himself there too. I want to know who we are in the beautiful sculpture that God has made.

My Prayer...

Hear my prayer, O God, to live in a world where everyone treats me like a neighbor and where I treat everyone like a neighbor. When I set the table tonight, let me set it well, as though all the people you love will be there, even me. In the name of Jesus Christ I pray. Amen.

CHAPTER THIRTY-TWO

Believing in Angels

God will command the angels concerning you to guard you in all your ways. On their hands they will bear you up, so that you will not dash your foot against a stone (Psalm 91:11,12).

There is no experience like being alone, and robbed, in a foreign country. God sends "angels" under these circumstances to restore us. I was on vacation, trying to travel "across" Ireland with my eight-year-old daughter Katie. It started to rain heavily. We drove to Dublin and checked into a B and B. It was late in the day and we had wanted to take in a play if we got to the city.

We made a fatal "un-savvy traveler" mistake. I did not unload my new and precious gift of a Coach purse of airline tickets, traveler's checks, passports, and jewelry when we arrived. We just went out quickly to make the eight o'clock performance.

On our two-block walk, we were mugged by a skinny kid who jumped on my back and stole my purse.

On the way over on Aer Lingus, Katie had said, "What

if the plane crashes?" I had said there was no chance because my angels were riding on my shoulders. In the event of an unlikely sea landing, they had the strength to hold the plane up. She had accepted their strength and my hyperbole.

When we got to the Dublin police station that night, and reported our rather complete loss, including the key to the B and B, Katie said, "Some angels."

She couldn't have been more right. We were able to find and wake the owner of the B and B, who lived in a Dublin suburb. He gave us some money, drove us to the airport, and put us on the next plane home, which plane accepted our story without question.

Some angels. They guard us when we are alone and transform loneliness into calm solitude.

My Prayer...

Good and gracious God, forgive those who mug people because they think they have no other way to eat or live. Forgive those who are foolish and make little mistakes that have big consequences. And forgive anyone who begins to doubt your angels. Wise them up, in Jesus' name. Amen.

CHAPTER THIRTY-THREE

Jesus Was Fully Present

And Pilate said to them, "Why, what evil has he done?" (Mark 15:14).

Jesus enters the city of Jerusalem humbly, knowing that people are out to get him. He enters in a kind of deep solitude that most of us pray for and long for. We too have enemies. We want to be calm in the face of them. We don't quite make it, but we try.

My son went with me to the wood pile. From it, I grabbed a particularly gnarled piece. Isaac grabbed it back and said, "No don't burn that one. I keep that one. It reminds me of Jimmy." Jimmy is the boy in his class who is also paraplegic. "I never want to burn that one," he said.

Isaac showed me the way to calm, and Jesus knew this method too. He loved more than he feared. He picked out pieces of wood, and certain people, and he focused on his love for them. He never wanted any of them burned, so he let himself go in their place.

This is the kind of love that John speaks of: "For God so loved the world…" This love is a focus on something other than ourselves and our enemies and what our enemies might do to us. Pilate recognized this love; he saw that Jesus' love was not dangerous, that it was actually liberating. From Jesus' love came the calm to ride on a donkey into the middle of the city. That calm created his constituency and got him killed. People in power knew its power, and they feared it.

Jesus was fully present in his Palm Sunday moment. Most of us live in packed time. We are living on too many levels at once. We are worrying about what we didn't do yesterday or what we must get done by tomorrow. We are not "here." We are not at home in here. We are "there," in anxiety. We could instead live in the knowledge of how greatly and deeply we are loved—but we aren't "here."

Jesus loves the gnarled pieces and the perfect pieces. He focused on that love and in that focus lost his fear of his enemies. What evil did he do? None.

How do we become "perfect" in this way? How do we become so completely ourselves that we don't miss the chance to love or save something? We have to use Jesus' strategy and steal time back, remove some of the obstacles in our way. Maureen Brady once said, "Whatever lies before me is not blocking my next step: it is my next step." One step at a time, one difficulty at a time, one recommitment at a time, that's how we have to do it.

My Prayer…

When fear overtakes me, O God, please calm me. Bring me to full presence when and where I am, obstacles and all. And there let me love others as I have been loved by you. Amen.

CHAPTER THIRTY-FOUR

The Paradox of Faith

I consider that the sufferings of this present time are not worth comparing with the glory about to be revealed to us (Romans 8:18).

St. Paul is saying here that what we suffer now is nothing compared to what is to come. But we don't believe that for a minute! We are the most overstimulated people who have ever lived, and we don't have time or tolerance for suffering. Instead, we have a constant need for adventure and excitement. Suffering has no place in our scheme of things.

Imagine how this attitude plays out for people who have suffered great losses, like the people in Oklahoma City after the bomb took their friends and their peace away. We want more excitement in our lives. They want less.

Faith is a conundrum because it moves us toward peace and excitement simultaneously. It demands that we experience both quiet and activity. It calls us to reflection in the midst of chaos. What happens in the middle of these emotions is resurrection. We rise in and out of our loneliness, in and out of our solitude. We should expect these "mood swings." Instead of accepting these changes from high to low, many people get lost. They lack the necessary rituals of faith to guide them. We learn from Scripture that low points in our lives often lead to the most productive periods in our lives. This is the paradox of our Christian faith. This is the paradox of the cross, and the cross leads to resurrection.

My Prayer...

O God, let me see through my difficulties to the time when I will once again experience your calm. Let me see beyond my own need and greed. Let me learn the rhythm of faith that teaches me to accept both the ups and the downs of my life. Amen.

CHAPTER THIRTY-FIVE

Believing in Miracles

But of that day or hour, no one knows. Therefore, watch, keep awake... keep alert (Mark 13:33, 35).

Many of us are familiar with and enjoy C.S. Lewis, the man who created the fictional land of Narnia. Lewis talks about being awake to possibilities and looking for the doors that get us from the common life to the uncommon life. We are to look around every corner, as though God (or Aslan, the great lion in the Lewis series who represents Jesus), might just be about to appear.

We may be so deep inside our own selves that we imagine there is no one there with us, or no one who could even find us. Lewis argues that Aslan (Christ) gets through the doors we shut to hold ourselves in

In *The Man Who Created Narnia: The Story of C.S. Lewis* by Michael Coren (Eerdmans, 1996), we hear how Lewis was awake enough himself to watch for God. He didn't bother with what most of us think of as success.

He lived an ordinary life in an extraordinary way. He went from common to uncommon through a set of simple doors. Associates at Oxford and Cambridge always wondered why he didn't make "more" of himself (p. 35). Why would he need to? He was already met by God. Where else was there to go?

Inspiration for the now famous wardrobe through which Edmund, Peter, Susan, and Lucy escape to Narnia (and return home safely) came to Lewis after harboring children from London during the war. One of the boys asked what would happen if you went in the wardrobe and tried to come out the other side. Lewis saved that image until mid-life—and put the great Christ-Lion on the other side.

In his letters, Lewis said, "It is quite useless knocking on the door of heaven for earthly comfort; it's not the sort of comfort they supply there." Lewis' solitude helped him understand that we are meant to be with God. He ends the Narnia chronicles with the children asking, "'Dare we? Can it be meant for us?' But while they were standing thus a great horn, wonderfully loud and sweet, blew from somewhere inside that walled garden and the gates swung open."

Lewis opened doors for many people. And he believed in miracles. He urged people to let themselves experience wonder and awe. Like his great friend and rival, Tolkien, he believed in things that most people don't regularly see. He saw the "deeper magic."

We, too, can see the deeper magic but we must stay awake for it. When we feel locked inside ourselves, as if someone has thrown away the key, think "doors." Think about the people who don't bother making "more" of themselves. They watch for God and for the deeper magic. They have the gift of solitude.

My Prayer

Keep me awake, O God, that I may not miss a minute of your wonders. Prepare me for the great horn, "wonderfully loud and sweet," and may I look for signs of it already here on earth. Amen.

Of Related Interest

Psalms for Times of Trouble

JOHN CARMODY

The author is openly realistic in this book of prayers forged in the darkness and trouble of his own battle with terminal cancer. Yet throughout there is a hope of the eternal kindness and mercy of God. A beautiful book to give to people in pain or sorrow.

ISBN: 0-89622-614-X, 168 pp, $9.95

Healing Wounded Emotions

Overcoming Life's Hurts

MARTIN PADOVANI

The author, a priest-counselor, describes how our emotional and spiritual lives interact and challenges readers to live fuller, more satisfying lives. People involved in counseling will find this a valuable handbook, and individuals with psychological and religious conflicts will find guidance to resolve conflicts and foster peace.

ISBN: 0-89622-333-7, 128 pp, $7.95
Audiobook: Three, 60-minute cassettes, $24.95
(order A-44)

Plucking the Strings... A Personal Psalm Journal

JOAN METZNER

The author invites you to allow God to pluck the strings of your heart and listen more deeply to its inner stirrings. She gives practical suggestions on how to prepare oneself physically and mentally for this spiritual exercise, and offers a question or brief reflection after each poetic psalm. Provides space for writing down personal thoughts and feelings. This book is perfect for use on retreat, morning or evening prayer, or any time set aside for prayer.

ISBN: 0-89622-733-2, 128 pages, $9.95

The Pummeled Heart

Finding Peace Through Pain

ANTOINETTE BOSCO

This touching story of one woman's struggle with many forms of suffering offers a model of how trust and hope in God gives strength for life's journey.

ISBN: 0-89622-584-4, 144 pp, $7.95

Available at religious bookstores or from:

TWENTY-THIRD PUBLICATIONS

P.O. BOX 180 • 185 WILLOW ST. • MYSTIC, CT 06355 • 1-860-536-2611 • 1-800-321-0411 • FAX 1-860-572-0788

Call for a free catalog